fresh start

The New Believer's Handbook

By Pastor Erik Lawson

Paperback ISBN-13: 979-8-9868682-4-0

First edition published in 2024.
Published in the United States.

Visit the author's website at: www.eriklawson.com

Published by 415 Leadership Inc.
100 Mall Parkway, Suite 500
Wentzville, Missouri 63385

fresh start

Table of Contents

How to Use This Booklet

Congratulations on your decision to receive Jesus Christ as your Lord and Savior or recommit your life to Him. It is the single most important decision that you will make in your entire life. This guide will give you the basics of the faith and help you build a strong foundation for your life. I encourage you to read a chapter and take time to reflect and take notes. Then, make some practical goals to implement what you have learned into your life. Be sure that your goals have a reasonable deadline from implementation. Our prayer for you is that you fulfill God's highest and best for your life.

Date I committed or recommitted my life to Christ: _____

Date I was baptized after committing my life to Christ: _____

Date I started serving: _____

Introduction

Welcome to your new life in Christ. I guarantee you, if you stick with your decision to follow Jesus, whether it's your first time or if it was a rededication, you'll discover that it is the best decision you have ever made. You'll find that when you truly follow Him with your whole heart, your life will become an epic and fulfilling adventure.

Let's begin by looking at your decision to follow Jesus in the context of the life of Christ. When Jesus began His ministry at 30 years of age, He was walking along the seaside of Galilee, and He saw some men that were fishing: Peter, Andrew, James, and John. He said to them,

> "Come follow me." ~ *Matthew 4:19 New International Version (NIV)*

They left their nets and followed Jesus. Christianity can be summarized this way; we're first and foremost called to be followers of Christ.

A foundation is a critical part of any house or building structure. If the foundation isn't right, it will eventually affect every other part of that building. Years ago, I actually had a home that had some structural problems in the foundation.

1

fresh start

Over time, the foundation began to crack under the surface. Then, cracks started to show up all over the place in the rooms above. Unfortunately, it cost me thousands of dollars to have that repaired.

This is much like your walk with Christ. If you don't get some of the foundational parts right in the beginning or skip certain fundamental truths and fail to apply them to your life, over time the cracks will begin to show up in many areas of your life. These cracks in your foundation might show up in your relationships, attitudes, a temptation you are seemingly unable to overcome, and in any number of other forms.

Jesus taught a parable in the Sermon on the Mount. This was His first publicly recorded sermon. He actually ended emphasizing the importance of a strong foundation. He relates a story of two men who each built a house. The first one was not a wise builder because he didn't take the time to dig down and create a strong foundation. This man heard the Word of God, but he failed to do what it said, and it was compared to building the house on sand. When the storms came, his house was washed away. The other man was wise, he not only heard the Word of God, but he actively applied it in his life. Jesus compared that to a man who dug deep and built his house on a foundation of rock. The storms came to that man's life too. Problems and negative circumstances come to everyone's life, but this man's house, his life, and work were built

2

on a strong foundation, it withstood the storms of life. The difference between these two men was one thing, their foundation. Our desire is to help you build your life on a solid foundation so that someday when you stand before Jesus, you will hear Him say...

"Well done, my good and faithful servant. You have been faithful in handling this small amount, so now I will give you many more responsibilities. Let's celebrate together!" ~ *Matthew 25:21 New Living Translation (NLT)*

Chapter 1

The Good News, the Bad News, and the Really Good News

The Good News

In a world filled with bad news isn't it refreshing to hear some good news? I am so glad to tell you, that's exactly why Jesus came. He came to give us good news. The good news of Jesus is you're free from sin and shame, plus as a bonus He's given you the power of God to walk in His ways.

The Apostle Paul wrote about two thirds of the books found in the New Testament. These were actually letters written to various churches of the day. He wrote this to the church in Rome.

> For I am not ashamed of the gospel of Christ, for it is the power of God to salvation for everyone who believes. ~ *Romans 1:16 New King James Version (NKJV)*

The New Testament was written in Greek. The word "gospel" comes from the Greek word, "evangelion" which means evangelism. It actually is really the first term for evangelist.

In the past, people didn't take baths often, because they didn't have access to running water. So, people might go weeks, months, or in some cases years without bathing. Imagine what that would be like in a hot climate. As you might guess, people were very stinky. The evangelist would come into town yelling, "Good news!" Why did they yell 'good news,' because they were selling soap, and to a society that was very stinky, soap was very good news.

What a great analogy to our life before Jesus, because sin stinks. If your marriage, other relationships, or any other part of your life stinks, you can usually trace it back to sin. The good news of the gospel is Jesus came to deal with the sin that causes our life to stink. That's the good news of the Gospel.

The word "power" that the Apostle Paul used in that verse, in the Greek, means "dunamis." That's literally where we get the word dynamite. God's word is different from other books, it is not just ink on paper. It is supernatural. It's the power of God to literally transform your life.

Let's go back to Romans 1:16 and look at the word salvation in that verse. That word into Greek is "sozo," which means to save entirely, to save completely. It's the complete package, because Jesus cares about every single part of your life. Jesus didn't just come so you could be saved from Hell and go to Heaven. Yes, that's part of the good news, but He cares about every part of your life, spirit, soul, and body in this life as well.

This is what Jesus has to say about your life.

> The thief's purpose is to steal and kill and destroy. My purpose is to give them a rich and satisfying life. ~ *John 10:10 (NLT)*

Jesus didn't just come to give you a little bit of life and a little bit of joy, Jesus came to bring vibrant life to every single part of your world. Jesus did not promise you a trouble-free life either. In John 16:33, He explained this for us.

> I have told you all this so that you may have peace in me. Here on earth you will have many trials and sorrows. But take heart, because I have overcome the world. ~ *John 16:33 (NLT)*

This side of heaven, you will have problems—guaranteed. Everyone does, so be forewarned. As a new believer this can trip you up and deceive you into thinking God doesn't have your back, has given up on you, or has stopped loving you. It can cause you to compare yourself to others, until you begin to think God is unfair. This is that thief from John 10:10 trying to fill you with doubts to get you to quit on your walk with Jesus. Remember, even if this seems like bad news, Jesus encourages us to take heart, because He has overcome this world. Tuck that into your arsenal for next time trouble comes your ways.

The Bad News and the Really Good News

I know I never fully appreciate good news until I know the bad news. When you understand how bad the bad news actually is, then it gives you a great appreciation for how great and awesome the good news is. We're about to look at what Jesus saved us from by His death on the cross and His resurrection.

Most people in our culture think all you have to do to get to Heaven is to be a good person. So, define a good person. As you think of your definition, let's see what God has to say on this topic, and what the Bible says about the plan of salvation. The overall plan comes from the book of Romans, and it's sometimes called the Romans Road. It's like a Cliff Notes version of God's plan of salvation. It really helps you understand why none of us are good enough to get into Heaven on our own merit, or by our own works. In Romans Paul gives you some insight into everyone's spiritual state.

> For everyone has sinned; we all fall short of God's glorious standard. ~ *Romans 3:23 (NLT)*

That word "all" means everyone, no one is left out. In fact, the entirety of Romans Chapter three is unpacking how none seek after God. You didn't seek after God, God sought you. You just simply

8

said, "Yes." The Bible is very clear on your unrighteous state before you are saved.

As the Scriptures say,

> There is no one righteous, not even one.
> ~ *Romans 3:10 (NIV)*

> The human heart is the most deceitful of all things, and desperately wicked. Who really knows how bad it is? ~ *Jeremiah 17:9 (NLT)*

The reality is, contrary to your opinion, none of us are good enough to get into Heaven. So, in the Old Testament, God spoke through His servant Moses and gave the law. There were 613 commandments in the law. These were boiled down by God into what we know as The 10 Commandments found in the book of Exodus chapter 20. It wasn't that you could get to Heaven by keeping the law, it was given to show that you could never be perfect and good enough to get to Heaven.

Let's look at five of The 10 Commandments from Exodus 20 as a self-inventory to see how good you actually are.

> You shall have no other gods before Me.
> ~ *Exodus 20:3 (NKJV)*

An idol, or God, can be anything that you put before God. This can be a person, money, a career, or any number of other things. Anything you love more than God, is your god. How can you tell if it is an idol? Ask yourself, "What do I trust in when I'm in a crisis?"

How about this one?

> You shall not murder. ~ *Exodus 20:14 (NIV)*

You probably are thinking, "I haven't broken that one." This is what Jesus had to say: being angry with another person is like committing murder in your heart (Matthew 5:21-23 paraphrased.) Look, we've all committed murder in of our heart with someone. We just haven't acted on it.

Here's another one:

> You shall not commit adultery. ~ *Exodus 20:14 (NKJV)*

Jesus said,

> But I say to you that whoever looks at a woman to lust for her has already committed adultery with her in his heart. ~ *Matthew 5:28 (NKJV)*

Adultery or any immorality isn't just an action. It's really the intent of the heart. Look, we've all committed sins in our heart that maybe we didn't act out on, because we didn't want the consequences.

Next:

> You must not testify falsely against your neighbor. ~ *Exodus 20:16 (NLT)*

What does that mean? When you gossip, when you tell half-truths about somebody to stab them in the back, or hurt their reputation, that's called gossip. We've all violated that verse. Often our social media accounts can reflect this one.

Last but not least:

> You shall not covet your neighbor's house; you shall not covet your neighbor's wife, nor his male servant, nor his female servant, nor his ox, nor his donkey, nor anything that *is* your neighbor's. ~ *Exodus 20:17 (NKJV)*

If you're overwhelmed with consumer credit card debt, what is that? It's buying things you can't afford to impress people that don't matter. Unfortunately, we live in a culture based on coveting. The truth is most of us already have much more than we need.

How did you do? I'm sure you found yourself guilty of one or more and that's just five out of ten. We've all broken God's law. It was given to convince us that we are all in need of a Savior, because it is impossible to save ourselves. Now that you know you need a Savior, let's move on to see exactly what we've been saved from.

About now, you're probably asking yourself, "So, if I can't earn Heaven, if I am not good enough to earn salvation, then what is it that I do earn?" Well, the Bible actually answers that in the book of Romans.

> For the wages of sin is death. ~ *Romans 6:23 (NLT)*

What are wages? They are something you earn, and you earned death. Death is spiritual separation from God. When Adam and Eve committed the first sin in the Garden of Eden by eating that forbidden fruit, physical death came into the earth, but death is not just physical, it's spiritual as well, meaning separation from God in Hell. Jesus came to save you from a literal place called Hell.

The Bible references Hell over 167 times. Jesus talked about Hell 33 different times. In fact, Jesus referenced Hell more than He did Heaven. Why? Because sin and the consequences of sin is a serious and an eternally deadly matter.

Many people struggle with the concept that a loving God could send anybody to Hell. God is love. In fact, God is so loving, that He doesn't send anyone to Hell. He gives people the freedom of choice. You get to choose if you go to Heaven or Hell. God gave you something called free will. He didn't want robots. He wanted people who would choose to love and follow Him willingly.

fresh start

If I had walked up to Sunny, my wife, when I first met her, and said, "You're going to love me and marry me." If I forced that on her, would that be love? Love that's not given a choice is not love at all. God isn't going to force you to love Him or serve Him. You have freedom of choice to reject Him. The problem is when you reject Him, the alternative is not very good. That alternative is separation from Him in a literal place called Hell.

God is also a just judge. Many of us wear different hats in of our daily lives. I'm a husband, a father, a boss, and a friend; we all have different hats. It doesn't change who I am as a person, there's just different hats that I put on at different times, and I'm all those things. Now, God is a good and loving God, and as a good loving God, He's also a just God, and He's the just judge of all the Universe. A just judge has to deal with crimes, criminals, and things that are a danger to society. What would you think if someone committed a terrible crime against you or a family member and when it went to court the judge just smiled and said, "I just love everybody," and then looked at the one who committed the crime and said, "You're free to go." No consequence. No justice. You intuitively know that's wrong. How would you feel?

Well, God is a righteous judge and because of that, He has to judge sin. Fortunately for you, Jesus took all the consequences and all the penalty for your sin that you deserved. He took God's wrath, and your punishment. He did that

13

for everyone who chooses to accept His sacrifice. However, if you reject His sacrifice, if you say, "No thanks Jesus, I don't want You as my Lord." Then, you're the one who has to pay for your sins. Just what does that mean and how bad is it? Keep reading to find out.

We've looked at the word Hell, and how Jesus spoke more about Hell than He did Heaven. So, what is Hell and how bad is it? The best summary of Hell is that it is the absence of God. Let's be clear, Hell is not a place God sends people, it is a place that people choose.

Hell is reserved for the person who intentionally rejects God. It is for that person who spends their entire life saying, "God, I don't want you. I don't want you to be my Savior. I am Lord. I don't want you to tell me how to live my life. I want to be my own god, make my own choices, and do it my own way." So, at the end of that person's life, God says, "I'm going to answer the prayer you've been praying your entire life. I'm giving you eternity without Me."

The reason Hell is so bad is because when you remove God, you remove everything that is good. God is light, Hell is complete utter darkness. In Hell you've lost the light of the world, Jesus (*John 8:12*). Did you know that Hell is eternal hunger? Why? Because Jesus said that He is the bread of life (*John 6:35*). Hell is an eternal state of thirst. Jesus tells the story about a man named Lazarus who was in Hell. He

14

desired just a single drop of water on his tongue to cool the flames and quench his thirst. Why? Jesus is the living water. ~ *John 7:38.* He said, "He who drinks of me will never thirst again." Hell is a place of eternal torment, because there is no peace. Why? Jesus is the Prince of Peace. ~ *Isaiah 9:6 (NIV).* There is no joy in Hell because Jesus is joy, "In Your presence is fullness of joy." ~ *Psalm 16:11 (NKJV).*

You may be thinking, "I don't believe in Hell or that it's a literal place." **What you and I believe doesn't change reality.** It might change our behavior, or our perception of reality, but it doesn't change the facts or reality.

If I were to go to the top a very tall building and jump off because I don't believe in gravity, and I think it's just a ploy to limit my life and control me, I'd find out fast the reality of gravity. What you and I believe about God doesn't change the reality of God. Our beliefs don't change God, but our beliefs will change us.

There was a famous mathematician many centuries ago, his name was Pascal. He often would debate others about the existence of God, the claims of Christ and salvation. He said something really wise, and it's been coined as Pascal's wager. He said, "If I'm wrong about my belief in Christ and God and I come to the end of my life and die and I cease to exist, I lose nothing. But, if I'm right and the claims of Christ

15

are true and you're wrong and there is a Heaven and there is a Hell, then you've lost everything."

Are you ready for the really good news? We looked at, "The wages of sin is death," and we saw it's the bad news. Now, we have a great appreciation for the Good News. Let's continue to look at Romans 6:23 because it didn't stop at, "For the wages of sin is death," period, exclamation point. The great news is that verse continues. There's a conjunction there, and it's the word "but," and it is the best looking, "but" you have ever seen, trust me.

> For the wages of sin is death, **but** the free gift of God is eternal life through Christ Jesus our Lord. ~ *Romans 6:23 (NLT)*

Jesus Christ is God's gift to you. That word salvation in the Greek is "sozo." It means complete and entire—the complete package. You might wonder, "Why was Jesus crucified, why did He have to die for my sins to be forgiven?" Sometimes you hear the cross referred to as a tree. Jesus had to die that way because that's where salvation was lost. Adam and Eve in the Garden of Eden allowed sin into this world at a tree by eating the forbidden fruit. Relationship with God was lost at a tree in a garden, and Jesus restored it on another tree in a garden. Jesus Christ, your Savior, took the penalty for your sins when He hung on that cross, so that through Him, you can be forgiven. That is very, very good news.

Chapter 2

Understanding Salvation

As you journey with Christ, there are two words that you will hear quite often. These words are mercy and grace. Let's look at what the Bible has to say on this topic.

> God saved you by his grace when you believed. And you can't take credit for this; it is a gift from God. Salvation is not a reward for the good things we have done, so none of us can boast about it. For we are God's masterpiece. He has created us anew in Christ Jesus, so we can do the good things he planned for us long ago. ~ *Ephesians 2:8-10 (NLT)*

What is mercy? Mercy is not getting what you do deserve. Grace on the other hand is getting what you don't deserve.

The book of Lamentations chapter three says,

> Because of the Lord's faithful love we do not perish, for His mercies never end. They are new every morning; great is Your faithfulness! ~ *Lamentations 3:22-*

fresh start

23 Holman Christian Standard Bible (HCSB)

Why every morning? Because you use them up every day, so your loving God gives you a do-over, fresh start each and every day. Everything you have in your life that is good is because God didn't give you what you deserved, which is Hell. You're saved by His grace. Now, this verse also says you were saved for something. You aren't saved by your good works because we could never do enough of those. You're saved for good works, and this is an important distinction. This is where many Christians early in their walk get mixed up and think their salvation depends on their good works. We're saved by grace, but we're saved for good works.

Now that we have an overview of the gospel, the good news. You know that salvation is a free gift. The question is how do you receive this free gift? You may have already received God's free gift of salvation but are struggling with doubts of how it all works. So, let's explore it.

> That if you confess with your mouth the Lord Jesus and believe in your heart that God has raised Him from the dead, you will be saved. ~ *Romans 10:9 (NKJV)*

Salvation is as simple as two things, it's what you confess with your mouth and what you believe in your heart. Notice, what's missing in the Scripture is any mention of the mind or emotions. These two aspects of your humanity can easily lead you astray with feelings of doubt and reasoning. Salvation is not a feeling or an intellectual decision, it comes from your spirit. Often in Scripture, references to the heart are connected to the spirit.

When you confess Jesus as your Savior, and believe in your heart God raised Him from the dead, it is similar to verbally signing a contract saying, "from here on Jesus I'm making you my Lord." Instead of using a pen and signing on paper, you're using your tongue. That word "believe" does not just mean to give mental assent or agreement, it means to fully depend, rely, lean upon.

Here's what Jesus did for you. There was a great divide between Heaven and Hell that you had no way to cross. He bridged it for you. He promises if you'll trust in what He did, and trust in Him as your Savior, He will get you across the divide.

Maybe you picked up this little booklet out of curiosity, but now you're at a point where you say, "I want this free gift." Or you're someone who at one point gave your life to Christ, but you've wandered and got off track. Today you can rededicate your life to the Lord. Or maybe you just need assurance that you're really saved. Simply pray this prayer out loud and mean it.

> Father,
>
> Thank you for sending Your son Jesus to die on the cross and pay for my sins. I believe all my sins have been paid for by that sacrifice. I give my life to You to be my Lord and Savior. From this day on, I will follow You. Thank You for saving me! I look forward to the great things You have planned for me as I follow You.
>
> In Jesus' Name, Amen.

I want to congratulate you. You just prayed the greatest prayer you're ever going to pray. From this moment forward, you're on an incredible journey in your new life in Christ.

Be sure to record the date you made this commitment to God on page vi.

One question I've been asked a lot over the years is this, "How do I know I'm saved?" That's a great question. The Bible actually helps answer that for us. We're going to look at seven signs that we see in someone who is truly saved. You are not saved because of these seven things, but these are indicators that you've truly experienced life-change.

Here are some of the signs that let us know we are saved.

1. The Bible tells us we are saved.

> These things I have written to you who
> believe in the name of the Son of God,
> that you may know that you have eternal
> life, and that you may *continue* to believe
> in the name of the Son of God. ~ *1 John
> 5:13 (NKJV)*

Salvation is a fact, not a feeling. One function of
the Bible is to assure those who have accepted
Christ, and confessed Him as Savior, that they
are saved. There are times when I doubt my
salvation because I messed up or didn't feel
saved, but I go to the Word of God and it reminds
me of the fact that I confessed, and believed, and
that God saved me, in spite of me, not because
of how good I performed. This reassures me that
I'm saved and that's a fact, because the Bible told
me so. Remember, feelings are not facts, they
are just feelings, and you can't trust feelings to
be the truth.

2. The Holy Spirit tells us; we are a child of God.

There's someone you can believe, and that's the
Holy Spirit. The Holy Spirit is often represented
as a dove, the symbol of peace. The Holy Spirit
comes and brings peace into your life and
assurance to your heart that you belong to God's
family.

> For His Spirit joins with our spirit to affirm that we are God's children. ~ *Romans 8:16 (NLT)*

There's something referred to as the inward witness of the Holy Spirit. When something is right in your life, you have a peace that bypasses your mind, it comes from your spirit, and you know that you know when something is right. It's the inward witness of the Holy Spirit. There are times my mind might be thinking, "Am I really saved? Look at the bad week I've had!" Then, the Holy Spirit will give me a peace that only He can give, and I know I'm good with God.

3. When you sin, it bothers you.

> And you He made alive, who were dead in trespasses and sins, in which you once walked according to the course of this world, according to the prince of the power of the air, the spirit who now works in the sons of disobedience, among whom also we all once conducted ourselves in the lusts of the flesh, fulfilling the desires of the flesh and of the mind. ~ *Ephesians 2:1-3 (NKJV)*

Before I became a Christian, I did all sorts of things that were sinful, and I actually bragged about them. However, once I gave my life to Christ and became a new creation in Him, He changed my heart. The things that I used to enjoy that were sinful, suddenly had no appeal anymore, because I was made new in Christ.

4. We love other Christians.

You will begin to have a love for other Christians. You'll find you have a heart change toward them. Maybe you're like me and before you accepted Christ, you wanted nothing to do with Christians because they were weird, and you thought church was a waste of your time. However, when I gave my life to Christ, I suddenly wanted to go to church and be around those same people I once thought were weird. My heart just changed for the people of God. John tells us, that is a sign of being saved.

> We know that we have passed out of death into Life, because we love the brothers and sisters. He who does not love remains in [spiritual] death. ~ *1 John 3:14 Amplified Bible (AMP)*

5. We desire to serve others.

> Now when Jesus had come into Peter's house, He saw his wife's mother lying sick with a fever. So He touched her hand, and the fever left her. And she arose and served them. ~ *Matthew 8:14-15 (NKJV)*

When you're truly born-again your new heart wants to serve others. All of a sudden, you start thinking about how you can make a difference. You stop living just for yourself and your own selfish desires and realize that you're not the center of the Universe. The book of Isaiah records a conversation between God and Isaiah.

> Also, I heard the voice of the Lord, saying: "Whom shall I send, And who will go for Us?" Then I said, "Here *am* I! Send me."
> ~ *Isaiah 6:8 (NKJV)*

Someone whose life is touched by God will ultimately begin to say, "God, I'm willing, use me to make a difference!"

6. You tell others what Jesus did for you.

Mark 1:40-45 relates a story of a man with leprosy who came to Jesus asking if He was willing to heal him. Of course, Jesus said "Yes." He laid His hand on the man, and he was instantly healed. Leprosy was incurable in that day. It's a horrible disease that slowly eats away your flesh. In the Bible leprosy is always a picture of sin. The man was so overjoyed because of his healing, he went out and began telling everyone about what Jesus did for him.

> But the man went and spread the word, proclaiming to everyone what had happened. As a result, large crowds soon surrounded Jesus, and he couldn't publicly enter a town anywhere. ~ *Mark 1:45a (NLT)*

When you receive salvation and your new life in Christ, you can't help but tell others about how

Jesus saved you and forgave you of all your sins. You want everyone to experience the same joy and freedom you've experienced in Christ.

7. You love God.

> We love Him because He first loved us. ~
> 1 John 4:19 (NKJV)

For most of us, we don't come to God because of our great love for Him, we come because we don't want to go to Hell, and we want Him to fix what is broken in our lives. Then, we accept Christ and as we begin to experience His love for us and how amazing His mercy and grace are, we fall in love with Him. One of the signs of someone who has experienced salvation is they will begin to love God because they discover how much He loves them. We didn't get our life together to come to God, we just came as we were. He loved us where we were at, but loved us too much to leave us there.

Chapter 3

The New You—Who You Are in Christ

I think everyone at some point in their life asks themselves the deep and profound question, "What is the purpose of my life?" King Solomon asked himself that same question and he was known as the wealthiest and wisest man to ever live. He wrote three books of the Bible: Proverbs, Song of Solomon, and Ecclesiastes. The entire book of Ecclesiastes is Solomon's search for the meaning of life. In the end, this is what he found.

> And I set my heart to know wisdom and to know madness and folly. I perceived that this also is grasping for the wind. ~ *Ecclesiastes 1:17 (NKJV)*

Solomon tried to discover his purpose through six things, none of which fulfilled his quest. He tried philosophy, pleasure, parties, projects, prosperity, and power. None of those things gave him the fulfillment he was seeking. We come to the end of Solomon's journal, and he says,

> That's the whole story. Here now is my final conclusion: Fear God and obey his commands, for this is everyone's duty. God will judge us for everything we do,

including every secret thing, whether
good or bad. ~ *Ecclesiastes 12:13-14
(NLT)*

He summarizes the meaning of life this way:
Number one, is to know God, which involves
reverencing God, keeping His commandments,
and having an eternal mindset which means,
we're to live our life through the filter of one day
we're going to stand before God and give an
account of our life. **Number two, is to grow in
Christ**, and **Number three**, is to **show Christ**
to others by the way we live. These three things
are at the core reasons for everything we do at
Element Church.

Everything Jesus did was about us forming a
relationship with God. I like what the apostle Paul
says in Colossians.

> For in Christ lives all the fullness of God in
> a human body. ~ *Colossians 2:9 (NLT)*

To know Jesus is to know God. Our relationship
with God is the key to a full rich life. The closer
you are to Jesus, the fuller your life is. The farther
you are from Jesus, the emptier your life is. The
joy you're experiencing today is in direct
proportion to your proximity to Jesus. As new
believers, here's what you're supposed to do.

> Like newborn babies, you must crave pure
> spiritual milk so that you will grow into a

29

full experience of salvation. Cry out for
this nourishment. ~ *1 Peter 2:2 (NLT)*

When you give your life to Christ, it's like being a
newborn baby. "Born again," as Jesus described
it. When a baby's born, they need milk to grow.
Healthy babies grow. If you don't see your baby
growing, you know there is a problem. Part of the
purpose of life and being with Christ is growth. In
fact, much of your satisfaction and fulfillment
comes through growth. Think about it, when you
achieve a goal in your life, it gives you a sense of
accomplishment. God wired you that way. When
you grow in Christ you experience this same type
of fulfillment. It is a choice to grow. It is not how
long you've been a Christian that determines how
mature you are, it's how much you press into
knowing and growing in Jesus. When you choose
to grow, the third thing naturally happens, you
show Christ. God's joy and peace makes you like
a light that attracts those seeking change in their
own lives.

> No one lights a lamp and then puts it
> under a basket. Instead, a lamp is placed
> on a stand, where it gives light to
> everyone in the house. In the same way,
> let your good deeds shine out for all to
> see, so that everyone will praise your
> Heavenly Father. ~ *Matthew 5:15-16
> (NLT)*

God wants you to live life in such a way that the
lifestyle and the things that you do for Him and

for others cause people to see Jesus in you. This side of Heaven, we're the only Jesus people ever see.

So, does all this mean I'm saved because of what I do? Absolutely not. You are saved solely and completely by believing and confessing that Jesus died for your sins and God raised Him from the dead. When you receive Jesus as your Lord and Savior spiritually, you literally become new.

> Therefore, if anyone is in Christ [that is, grafted in, joined to Him by faith in Him as Savior], he is a new creature [reborn and renewed by the Holy Spirit]; the old things [the previous moral and spiritual condition] have passed away. Behold, new things have come [because spiritual awakening brings a new life]. ~ *2 Corinthians 5:17 (AMP)*

This means you're being given a complete do-over in Christ. Your past is literally erased in God's mind. You are His child, officially adopted into God's family. This is so important for you to believe. You see your spirit is born-again, but your body hasn't changed and your soul (mind, will, and emotions) still need some work.

For most of us, this is where the confusion comes in. When we gave our lives to Christ, our spirit was brought to life by the power of the Holy Spirit and now the new you is stuck living in the same body and the same mind, will, and emotions as the old you. We are a spirit, we have a soul (that's our mind, will, and emotions), and we live in a body.

> And you *He made alive*, who were dead in trespasses and sins, in which you once walked... ~ *Ephesians 2:1-2a (NKJV)*

This Scripture describes how God brought your spirit to life when you accepted Jesus.

Your spirit was dead and full of wickedness, but God changed all that and brought your spirit to life and made it pure and holy in His sight. The Bible refers to this as being a new creature or creation in Christ. All you did was confess and believe and God did the rest.

> Therefore, if anyone *is* in Christ, *he is* a new creation; old things have passed away; behold, all things have become new. ~ *2 Corinthians 5:17 (NKJV)*

So, now that my spirit is born-again, why do I seem to keep sinning?

Well, this gets back to the fact of what we said before, you're a new you in the same old body with the same old soul. When your body and your soul team up against your spirit, that's when you'll lose the battle and sin. The key is, as we walk with Jesus and learn about who we are as a new creature, we can begin to reprogram our wrong thinking so that our soul gets trained to line up with your spirit. When this happens you now have your spirit and soul teamed up against your body and you will make fewer and fewer choices to sin. Salvation is instantaneous, your spirit is as saved as it will ever be. However, training your soul and body is a process. So, be patient with yourself. This is how the Bible explains it.

> And I know that nothing good lives in me, that is, in my sinful nature. I want to do what is right, but I can't. ~ *Romans 7:18 (NLT)*

> And do not be conformed to this world, but be transformed by the renewing of your mind... ~ *Romans 12:2 (NKJV)*

We need to keep in mind that there is a difference between positional truth and practical truth.

My kids are Lawsons by position. They were born into it. However, in practiced truth, at times they didn't live up to my name, but that didn't change the positional truth that they are Lawsons.

The good news is, when you know and believe that you are a King's kid it changes the way you behave. To change your behavior, you must change what you believe. We struggle with the "do" because, we don't know the "who" we are in Him. The Apostle Paul says it this way in the book of Ephesians.

> Since you have heard about Jesus and have learned the truth that comes from

33

> him, throw off your old sinful nature and your former way of life, which is corrupted by lust and deception. Instead, let the Spirit renew your thoughts and attitudes. Put on your new nature, created to be like God—truly righteous and holy. ~ *Ephesians 4:21-24 (NLT)*

The bottom line is you have to change your mind to change your life. Your life is a by-product of your mind. A person's life is a collection of thoughts that they acted upon that created the life they are currently living. So, if your thought life has taken you to a place you'd prefer not to be, you need to change your thinking to get you to where you want to go.

According to the National Endowment for Financial Education, about 70% of the people who win the lottery or receive a large windfall go bankrupt within a few years.

This is a result of wrong thinking patterns about money. This same principle can apply to any area of our life. Most of us don't reflect upon what we are thinking about.

> We use God's mighty weapons, not worldly weapons, to knock down the strongholds of human reasoning and to destroy false arguments. We destroy every proud obstacle that keeps people from knowing God. We capture their

> rebellious thoughts and teach them to obey Christ. ~ *2 Corinthians 10:4-5 (NLT)*

In order to live a victorious Christian life, you'll need to start policing your thoughts like you were an MP at the gate of a top-secret installation making sure no enemies breached your facility. Research suggests that we think upwards of 50,000 thoughts a day and that 80% of these thoughts are repeats of yesterday's thoughts. To make matters worse, sadly, most of our self-talk in our thought realm is negative. Negative self-talk can take many forms. A common example is, "I'm not good enough." This can come as an articulated thought or nagging fear. 50,000 thoughts a day add up to a whooping 18,000,000 thoughts each year.

Your goal should be to stop any thoughts that do not line up with who God says you are. Capture those rebellious negative thoughts and make them obedient to Christ. Ask yourself, "Does this line up with what God says about me?" To answer this question, you'll need to equip yourself with the knowledge of what God says about you.

> Study this Book of Instruction (the Bible) continually. Meditate on it day and night so you will be sure to obey everything written in it. Only then will you prosper and succeed in all you do. ~ *Joshua 1:8 (NLT)*

You change your mind by changing what's in your mouth. Do you know that you believe more of what you hear yourself say than what any other person says? There is something in Scripture called meditation. Meditation in this context is not the kind found in Eastern Religions. It is a picture of an animal that chews its cud. According to Leviticus 11:3, not all cud chewing animals were clean to eat. According to Jewish law, the Jewish people were only allowed to eat animals that were considered clean. These animals had two distinguishing characteristics. They chewed the cud and they had cloven hoofs. As Christians, we are clean by how we walk and what we eat. This means, how we live our lives and what we say. This means, as Christians, we no longer live the way the world lives or speak and think the way the world does.

Isaac Newton's first law of motion states that: "Every object will remain at rest or in a state of uniform motion (in a straight line) unless compelled to change its state by the action of an external force."

To take Newton's statement from the scientific perspective and apply it to our lives on a practical level, we can put it this way: successful people do consistently what others do occasionally.

At 15, I gave my life to Jesus in front of a movie theater. I felt renewed and excited. However, by the next day the feelings wore off and I reverted to my old way of seeing myself. The devil convinced me that I was not saved. Three months later I once again gave my life to Christ. In fact, for months, every time the pastor gave an altar call, I would give my life to Christ again. Then, one day the pastor explained to me that salvation is not a feeling. He asked me two questions, "Do the sinful things you used to love to do now bring you guilt instead of pleasure? Second, "Do the things you used to love to do that were ungodly, now you have no desire to do those things anymore? In fact, you hate the thought that you ever did them." I answered, "Yes" to both those questions. Then, the pastor said, "Erik those are both signs that God has changed your heart, and you are saved." That was a light bulb moment for me, and I've never looked back since. That lie lost its grip on my life.

We've talked about the fact that we change our mind by changing what we say, and we need to go to God's Word to find out who God says we are so we can make that change. So, here are just a few of the things God says you are, not somewhere in the future, but now, and God cannot lie.

There's an old song called the *Great Adventure*. One of the lines in the song is, "I opened up my Bible and read about me. I once was a prisoner and now I am free." Let's open up the Bible and find out what it says about you.

fresh start

You are forgiven.

> He is so rich in kindness and grace that he purchased our freedom with the blood of his Son and forgave our sins. ~ *Ephesians 1:7 (NLT)*

You are chosen, royal, and holy.

> But you *are* a chosen generation, a royal priesthood, a holy nation, His own special people, that you may proclaim the praises of Him who called you out of darkness into His marvelous light. ~ *1 Peter 2:9 (NKJV)*

You are His masterpiece.

> For we are God's masterpiece. He has created us anew in Christ Jesus, so we can do the good things he planned for us long ago. ~ *Ephesians 2:10 (NLT)*

You are His heir.

> And since we are his children, we are his heirs. In fact, together with Christ we are heirs of God's glory. ~ *Romans 8:17 (NLT)*

You are righteous.

> For He made Him who knew no sin *to be* sin for us, that we might become the righteousness of God in Him. ~ *2 Corinthians 5:21 (NKJV)*

You are free.

> And because you belong to him, the power of the life-giving Spirit has freed you from the power of sin that leads to death. ~ *Romans 8:2 (NLT)*

You are complete.

> So you also are complete through your union with Christ, who is the head over every ruler and authority. ~ *Colossians 2:10 (NLT)*

You are an overcomer.

> But you belong to God, my dear children. You have already won a victory over those people, because the Spirit who lives in you is greater than the spirit who lives in the world. ~ *1 John 4:4 (NLT)*

This is just a fraction of the amazing things you are in Christ. As you read your Bible and listen to teaching, you will discover many more. I want to encourage you to memorize these Scriptures, so when thoughts of doubt come, you can use them to defeat the negative thoughts with the truth of what God says.

I want to leave this topic with these last important thoughts and Scriptures, because so often believers can fall into the misbelief that God has given up on them or is mad at them when they slip up or fail. Here are some vital things for you to know. God loves you not because of anything you do or don't do, but because He is good and His love for you is unconditional.

Jesus understands you, and nothing can make Him stop loving you, so we have no need to fear.

> This High Priest of ours understands our weaknesses, for he faced all of the same testings we do, yet he did not sin. So let us come boldly to the throne of our gracious God. There we will receive his mercy, and we will find grace to help us when we need it most. ~ *Hebrews 4:15-16 (NLT)*

> And I am convinced that nothing can ever separate us from God's love. Neither death nor life, neither angels nor demons, neither our fears for today nor our worries about tomorrow—not even the powers of hell can separate us from God's love. No power in the sky above or in the earth below—indeed, nothing in all creation will ever be able to separate us from the love of God that is revealed in Christ Jesus our Lord. ~ *Romans 8:38-39 (NLT)*

Chapter 4

The Bible

Reading the Bible, often referred to as the Word of God or the Word, is the first and foremost way we get to know Christ, build a relationship with Him, and learn how to live as a Christian. Before we talk more about that, let's look at practical insights that will help give you an overall understanding of this book that was inspired by God to help us live our lives and fulfill our purpose.

The Bible is a collection of 66 books written by 40 different authors written over a 1,400-year period in three languages, on three continents. It is divided into two divisions: the Old Testament, Genesis through Malachi, and the New Testament, Matthew through Revelation.

The Old Testament is filled with the account of the creation, stories for living, poetry, hundreds of prophesies about the coming Messiah, Jesus, and books of wisdom such as Proverbs. The New Testament begins with four books about the life and ministry of Jesus here on the earth. These books are referred to as the Gospels: Matthew, Mark, Luke, and John. The book of Acts is about the beginning of the church, and is followed by the Epistles, which mean letters. These letters are from leaders of the early church to specific churches. Ephesians for example, was written by the Apostle Paul to the church at Ephesus. The last book of the Bible is Revelation which tells of the end times and the return of Christ and His Kingdom that will last forever.

Each book contains chapters and verses designated by numbers. Genesis 1:1 is the first chapter of the book of Genesis and the first verse.

> In the beginning God created the heavens and the earth. ~ *Genesis 1:1 (NKJV)*

The letters behind the chapter and verse designation indicate which version of the Bible is being quoted. In this case, NKJV stands for New King James Version.

God wants to speak to you and one of the main ways He does this is when you read the Bible. You can look at it this way, if you have a car, it came with a user manual that the company that designed and built the car created so you would know how to use and take care of the car and keep it running. God created us, and the Bible is His user manual for us, His creation. Jesus gave us a promise in John 10.

> My sheep hear My voice, and I know them, and they follow Me. ~ *John 10:27 (NKJV)*

In this Bible verse, Jesus is referring to a nomadic illustration or a metaphor. In Biblical times, when shepherds were grazing their flocks, there would be multiple flocks grazing in the same field. So how did the shepherds find their sheep? Actually, it was the sheep who knew which shepherd was theirs. Each shepherd had a song, a whistle, or a sound that they would make that was distinct to their individual herd. When it was time to leave, the shepherd would do their distinct call, and the sheep would recognize their shepherd's voice and follow the shepherd. We are given the promise that we could recognize the voice of Jesus so we can follow Him. The Bible is the number one way God uses to speak to us and give us guidance.

The gospel of John says,

> In the beginning was the Word, the Word was with God, and the Word was God. ~ *John 1:1 (NKJV)*

The Bible and God's words are inseparable. In fact, John 1:14 tells us Jesus is the Word.

> And the Word became flesh and dwelt among us, and we beheld His glory, the glory as of the only begotten of the Father, full of grace and truth. ~ *John 1:14 (NKJV)*

Spending time reading your Bible is literally spending time with God. It's God's voice and His word to you. We often hear, "I tried reading the Bible, but I don't understand it." First, consider starting off with a translation like the New Living

Translation. It is written in modern English and leaves out many archaic terms, that are unfamiliar within our culture. Read it prayerfully, ask God to speak to you as you read. The more you know Jesus, the more you will begin to understand the Bible, so stick with it even if it seems awkward at first. I recommend that you start with the Gospel of John.

You might be asking, "How do I know for sure that the Bible is really God's Word and that I can trust it?" I'm glad you asked. This is so important because how you view the Bible is how you view God, yourself, life, others, and the definition of right and wrong. You find all these things in your Bible. First, let's look at the trustworthiness of the Bible.

> All Scripture is inspired by God and is useful to teach us what is true and to make us realize what is wrong in our lives. It corrects us when we are wrong and teaches us to do what is right. God uses it to prepare and equip his people to do every good work. ~ *2 Timothy 3:16-17 (NLT)*

The Bible is not just a book of fables. In fact, it's not just ink on paper like other books, it is truly inspired and divinely authored by God. It is like oxygen to our soul. The Bible is unlike any other book in human history. Yes, it was written by flawed men; really the whole story of the Bible is God using flawed people to proclaim a perfect

God. Now, if God could create the heavens and the earth with just His Word, think of the magnitude of this scripture.

> Then God said, "Let there be light," and there was light. ~ *Genesis 1:3 (NLT)*

At his command, 200 billion—billion—stars and galaxies appeared. If God could create all that with just His Word, then it would make perfect sense that God could preserve His Word throughout the ages for us. That would be a very minor miracle in comparison to all the miracles of life that we encounter each and every day.

To help you understand why the Bible is different from any other book ever written, let's look at some historical context.

When we read the Old Testament, we see God established Judaism. It was the first monotheistic, meaning one God, world religion. Judaism cited one God in the form of three persons, the Father, Son, and Holy Spirit. This is where we get the doctrine of the Trinity. Our Christian roots are in Judaism and are the foundation of our faith. Jesus is from a Jewish background. His birth, ministry, death, and resurrection were predicted throughout the Old Testament.

This separated Judaism and Christianity from all other religions because the other religions were all polytheistic, meaning they worshipped multiple gods. These gods usually took the form of natural things like the sun, trees, animals, or even the Earth itself. Also, Judaism and Christianity were the first to cite that we were created in the image of God. What this did was in contrast to other world religions. It put a value on mankind. Every man, and every woman, regardless of race, or socio-economic status, have value because each person is made in the image of our Creator. Another thing that separates Judaism and Christianity from other religions is that they are the only religions that believe God wants a personal relationship with the mankind that He created. In other religions their gods are impersonal and removed from humanity.

Lastly, perhaps the most important thing that separates Christianity from any other religion, and the Bible from any other religious book, is other religions tell people how to become good enough. The Bible tells us we'll never be good enough. The Bible, and the story of individuals in it, show us that man is lost and in need of a Savior, because we can't save ourselves. So, God did what no one else could do. He came to save us in the person of Jesus Christ. **Religion is man's attempt to reach God; Christianity is God's attempt to reach man through the person of Jesus Christ.**

Now that we've looked at how important the Bible is and why we can trust it, let's go ahead and talk about how you can study this amazing book,

God's Word to you. Here are some quick practical things that will help you get the most of your time in the Bible. As you grow in your knowledge of your Bible, you will grow in the knowledge of God.

1. Be consistent. It is wiser to read a little each and every day rather than reading a large amount in one sitting and then not picking up your Bible for a month. This would be like eating a huge meal and expecting it to get you through the next 30 days. The Bible is food for our spirit. Commit to a daily appointment with God and your Bible. Put it on your calendar like you would a dinner engagement.

2. Talk to God about what it is you're reading. We often tend to read the Bible like a novel, quickly from beginning to end. The Bible is not just any book, and it wasn't designed for speed reading. It's better to stop and think about what you're reading. In fact, there is a word called "meditation" or "meditate" in the Hebrew language which literally means "to chew" like a cow chewing on its cud. When a cow eats, it chews on its food over and over and over. We are to chew on the Word of God.

So, read a passage and then do this: talk to God about it. "Okay, Lord, you just talked about this here. What does that mean to me? How am I doing with that? What do You want to speak to me about that specific passage?" One of the greatest forms of prayer is actually just talking to

God about His Word. When you don't know what to pray, read the Word to God.

When you're really seeking God, occasionally you'll find things you don't like. One of the functions of God's Word is to correct you when you need it. He might correct an attitude or behavior, even a motive. The most painless way to handle these situations is to thank Him for the correction and make the change, because it's for your own good. Don't justify your behavior, because God is always right, and He will always act in your best interest.

3. As you're reading, God will talk to you. There will be things that seem to jump off the page at you. They are "Ah, ha" moments! This is called a revelation. Keep a notebook and pen or electronic device with you when you read and write those things down. Also, don't be afraid to underline them in your Bible. From time to time, look back over your notes and refer back to the Scriptures that impacted you.

There's an account in the book of Acts where Paul is preaching to a group of people called the Bereans. He's telling them things that they had never heard before, so they were a bit skeptical. Here is what they did.

> And the people of Berea were more open-minded than those in Thessalonica, and they listened eagerly to Paul's message. They searched the Scriptures day after

day to see if Paul and Silas were teaching the truth. ~ *Acts 17:11 (NLT)*

When you're listening to a sermon or podcast, don't just take it at face value, go back, like the Bereans, and search the Scriptures to make sure that what was said is accurate.

Let's look at another important fact about the Bible. **The Bible is truth. It doesn't just have truth, it is truth.**

If you wanted to build a dream home first, you'd have an architect design it and create blueprints which give the builder all the specific measurements and details they need to construct the house. Then, you'd hire a contractor to build it. What if you hired laborers who all had their own ideas about measurements? One held to the standard that 12 inches is one foot. Another decided 18 inches was a foot, and another decided that 24 inches would equal one foot. How do you think your dream home would turn out?

Despite culture's push to declare there are no absolutes, there are absolutes that govern the world in which we live that God has established. There is such a thing as absolute truth. Here's what Jesus had to say about truth.

Jesus said to the people who believed in him, "You are truly my disciples if you remain faithful to my teachings. And you

49

> will know the truth, and the truth will set you free." ~ *John 8:31-32 (NLT)*

> Make them holy by your truth; teach them your word, which is truth. ~ *John 17:17 (NLT)*

> Jesus told him, "I am the way, the truth, and the life. No one can come to the Father except through me." ~ *John 14:6 (NLT)*

There are absolutes by which we should build our life. If we decide to determine our own truth, then the foundation of our life will be very shaky. There are two schools of thought today. One is individualism. Individualism says this: if it feels good, it can't be that bad or wrong. The problem is our prison systems are full of people who lived by the philosophy of individualism, "If it feels good, do it." That's how they got into prison. There are many things that people do that feel good, but ultimately, they hurt themselves and others. That is a really poor philosophy for living. If it feels good, it doesn't necessarily mean it is good and it doesn't necessarily mean it is truth by which we should govern our lives.

There's another school of thought and that is relativism which says, "Look, there really is no right or wrong, there are no absolutes. Don't judge me, I won't judge you." That is another shaky foundation to build your life on. What's interesting is the people who say there are no absolutes just made an absolute statement. So next time somebody tells you, "There are no absolutes," say, "Are you absolutely sure about that?"

Defining your own truth is a very dangerous way to live your life. The Bible is the truth. It's the standard that God set by which we should measure all the decisions that we make. It is the standard by which we determine what is right and wrong. **Truth doesn't change over time. Culture doesn't define truth. God defines truth.**

There is no way to deny that there are examples of absolutes in the world all around us. One of the most obvious examples is gravity. You can deny it and say I feel there's no such thing, but if you jump off a tall building, you will discover gravity is one of life's absolutes. Whether you believe in the absolute of gravity or not does not change the reality that it exists.

Throughout the Bible are absolute truths that God has established that should govern your life. Whether you believe in them or not doesn't change the reality of those truths.

The absolute truths of God's Word are like stop lights. You can ignore them. You can sincerely believe that red light is not really red, but you will have to suffer the consequences of that choice if you choose to run it. The world would be chaos if we did not have absolutes. The reason so many people's lives, relationships, finances, and kids are in chaos is because they're not living by the absolute standards of what God has defined as right and wrong. Proverbs has something to say about this.

> There is a path before each person that seems right, but it ends in death. ~ *Proverbs 14:12 (NLT)*

God put commandments and truth in His Word, not to restrict your life, but to empower your life.

Chapter 5

Prayer

The second way that we really get to know God and have a personal relationship with Him is through this privilege that we call prayer. So exactly how do you define prayer? Simply put, prayer is communicating with God. It is a dialogue, a two-way conversation. You talk. God listens. God talks. You listen. It's relationship. It's communication. Communication is the lifeblood of all relationships, and God wants to have a vibrant relationship with you.

The power of prayer is not found in the length of your prayer. When the disciples asked Jesus to teach them to pray, He gave them this 65-word sample prayer.

In this manner, therefore, pray:

Our Father in Heaven,
Hallowed be Your name.
Your kingdom come.
Your will be done
on earth as *it is* in heaven.
Give us today our daily bread.
And forgive us our debts,
as we forgive our debtors.
And do not bring us into temptation,

> But deliver us from the evil one.
> For Yours is the kingdom and the power
> and the glory forever. Amen. ~ *Matthew*
> *6:9-13 (NKJV)*

This prayer of Jesus also answers the question, who do I pray to? Do I pray to the Father, the Son, or the Holy Spirit? Jesus said, "Our Father in Heaven." He reconfirms that we are to pray to the Father in Jesus' name in John 16.

> At that time you won't need to ask me for anything. I tell you the truth, you will ask the Father directly, and he will grant your request because you use my name. You haven't done this before. Ask, using my name, and you will receive, and you will have abundant joy. ~ *John 16:23-24 (NLT)*

What is so special about Jesus' name? Honestly, for a long time, I had no idea. I'd hear everyone pray and they'd end their prayer, "In Jesus' Name, Amen." In Jesus' name I thought was a CB sign off—"Ten-four, good buddy." I also wondered if it was some type of spiritual password for, "Here are all my secret regrets—by the way—code word: In Jesus' Name, Amen."

That was completely wrong! The truth is, when we use the name of Jesus, we are using his credit! That is the good news—because our crew was short! We are using Jesus' credit line with the Father and not ours. Jesus is our American

Express Platinum credit line! So, we don't receive answers to prayers because we are worthy, we receive answers because He is worthy.

Sometimes we think prayer is a long and lofty string of big words peppered with thee and thou's. Nothing could be further from the truth. Think of it this way: picture your favorite person to hang out with. You love spending time with this person and today you're spending the entire day with them. As you go along, you say something and your friend answers you. There may be times during this day, you say nothing at all, you're just hanging together. Then, you see something that reminds you of something your friend did for you, and you thank your friend. Your friend says, "You're welcome, it was my pleasure." God wants to be your best friend. God wants to hang out with you every day 24/7.

When you're trying to reach God and it feels like there is no answer, or you're getting a busy signal, there's a reason. You may not be giving space for God to answer. It's like a walkie talkie. You press the button to talk, but you have to let go of the button to receive a message back. Sometimes you can get so busy giving God your "needs" list, you forget to take the time to let Him answer. If you're not careful you can find yourself treating Him like a vending machine rather than seeking a relationship with Him. You can also move so far from God that you're out of range and can't hear His answer. Did you know that God never moves away from you? However, you can move away from Him. His promise is this:

> Don't love money; be satisfied with what you have. For God has said, "I will never fail you. I will never abandon you." ~ *Hebrews 13:5 (NLT)*

The answer to this dilemma is found in Scripture.

> Come close to God, and God will come close to you. Wash your hands, you sinners; purify your hearts, for your loyalty is divided between God and the world. ~ *James 4:8 (NLT)*

When we're living more in the world than for God it creates a distance that makes it difficult to hear His voice. The answer is to turn around and go back to God as your source.

Another common temptation is to attempt to turn prayer into a formula. We think if I remind God of the right promise and quote the right Scripture, my answer will pop out like a cosmic vending machine. Prayer is not a formula to get things from God, and God is not your cosmic answered prayer vending machine. In fact, the New Testament records 37 different miracles performed by Jesus and He didn't do any of them exactly the same. I suspect that was to keep us from trying to create formulas. When you don't have a formula, it keeps you dependent on Him.

This allows God to move and do what only He can do.

Many times, what you think you need and ask for isn't really what you need at all. It's easy to tell God what you need. The problem is you don't see the big picture that God sees. God knows exactly what you need and honestly more times than not, it's not what you think you need. So, when you communicate with God it is wise to be direct, but you should not be directive, because you don't see the whole picture like God does. In your prayers, you need to leave room for God to be God. **The goal of prayer is more about holding the hand of God than it is moving the hand of God.**

While there are no formulas for prayer, we do see that prayer has ingredients. For example, in the 37 recorded miracles of Jesus, we consistently see that faith is a key ingredient to answered prayer. Here's just one example:

> Then He touched their eyes, saying, "According to your faith let it be to you."
> ~ Matthew 9:29 (NKJV)

You'll see this phrase. "According to your faith," repeatedly in the Scriptures. Faith is more than just acknowledging that God can do something, that is a fact—not faith. Faith is not just hoping either. However, hope is an important factor. Hebrews 11:1 gives us God's definition of faith.

> Now faith is the [a] substance of things hoped for, the [b] evidence of things not seen. ~ *Hebrews 11:1 (NKJV)*

Because God cannot lie, you can trust Him in every area of your life. He embodies integrity and honor. He is completely trustworthy.

> And this same God who takes care of me will supply all your needs from his glorious riches, which have been given to us in Christ Jesus. ~ *Philippians 4:19 (NLT)*

Because you know His character, you can confidently trust that if He said it, He will do it. Just remember not to put Him in a box. There are times you pray in faith for something, and it doesn't happen the way you envisioned. You might pray for someone for healing, and you don't see the answer you were expecting. If you are not careful, this can shake your faith. In times like these, you need to realize you're not seeing the whole picture that God sees, and you need to remind yourself that you serve a good God. If it's not good, then He's not done. He may answer differently than you expected, but you can have faith in the character of God. He is going to meet your needs. You can trust that, so it is as good as done. So, **faith is believing that I have what God said I would have.**

Let's look at a couple of technical things about prayer. You might be asking since God is three persons in one, do I pray to God the Father,

Jesus, or the Holy Spirit? Jesus answers this in the book of John in a conversation He has with His disciples before He went to the cross.

> At that time you won't need to ask me for anything. I tell you the truth, you will ask the Father directly, and he will grant your request because you use my name. ~ *John 16:23 (NLT)*

You are to direct your prayers to the Father in Jesus' Name and the Holy Spirit helps you to pray.

> And the Holy Spirit helps us in our weakness. For example, we don't know what God wants us to pray for. But the Holy Spirit prays for us with groanings that cannot be expressed in words. ~ *Romans 8:26 (NLT)*

Why do we pray this way? We are not coming to God on our own merit or righteousness. That would gain us nothing. We come to God the Father in Jesus' Name, because of His merit and righteousness. This way I'm not coming to the Father in my name, I'm coming in the name of His Son.

Will you get it all right? No. You will miss it now and then, but that's okay. God loves you and He is thrilled when you take the time to be with Him. Make Him the first person you talk to each morning. Make a date with Him each day and your day will be started on the right foundation. Make Him the last person you talk to each night before you drift off to sleep and converse with Him throughout the day. It may not change all your circumstances, but it will change your focus and perspective.

Chapter 6

Holy Spirit

A very, very important and essential doctrine of the Christian faith is the Trinity. We talked briefly about this in the section on the Bible. God is a triune, or three-part being, God the Father, God the Son, and God the Holy Spirit. These three are coequal, coeternal, and yet one God. They are three distinct persons, yet Scripture tells us there is one God. The word "trinity" is not found in of the Bible, but we see evidence of the Trinity woven all throughout Scripture.

> Hear O Israel, the Lord our God, the Lord *is* one! ~ *Deuteronomy 6:4 (NKJV)*

However, we see that there are three distinct persons inside of that one God. This is a difficult concept to grasp, so let's try to get some clarity. God created the first man in the first chapter of Genesis. This is what it says:

> Then God said, "Let Us make man in Our image, according to Our likeness." ~ *Genesis 1:26 (NKJV)*

Now, what we see is the use of plural pronouns, "Our likeness. Our image." Yet it's very clear there is one God, but we see Him using plural pronouns to describe Himself.

Now let's look in the New Testament. The third chapter of Matthew records the account of Jesus' baptism. We see that the Holy Spirit descends upon Jesus in the form of a dove. Then, we hear the voice of God the Father. So, we see the Trinity revealed here at the baptism of Jesus.

> When He had been baptized, Jesus came up immediately from the water; and behold, the heavens were opened to Him, and He saw the Spirit of God descending like a dove and alighting upon Him. And suddenly a voice *came* from heaven, saying, "This is My beloved Son, in whom I am well pleased." ~ *Matthew 3:16-17 (NKJV)*

In this Scripture, we clearly see the three persons of the Trinity, God the Father, God the Son (Jesus), and God the Holy Spirit, right there at baptism. Later, Jesus gives the Great Commission as He's preparing to go up into Heaven where we also see the three persons of the Godhead.

> Go therefore and make disciples of all nations, baptizing them in the name of the Father and of the Son and of the Holy Spirit. ~ *Matthew 28:19 (NKJV)*

So, we can confidently say, there is one God who reveals Himself in three persons. This is one of those things that none of us will probably fully understand this side of Heaven. The Bible even tells us in Isaiah that God is beyond our understanding.

> "For My thoughts *are* not your thoughts, Nor *are* your ways My ways," says the Lord. "For *as* the heavens are higher than the earth, So are My ways higher than your ways, And My thoughts than your thoughts." ~ *Isaiah 55:8-9 (NKJV)*

When St. Patrick was in Ireland telling the people about Jesus and salvation, he ran into a group of people who were trying to grasp the concept of the Trinity. He saw a three-leaf clover and picked it up. He said, "Each one of these leaves is still the same clover, but they're distinctly individual parts of that same clover." I guess you could say that was a pretty good example of the Trinity. I love what one theologian said, **"If God was small enough to understand, He wouldn't be big enough to worship."**

The Holy Spirit, the third person of the Godhead helps us get closer to Jesus. He is the helper Jesus sent us after He ascended to Heaven. Notice the Holy Spirit is a "he" not an "it." There is a big distinction between those two terms. Let's look at this further in Scripture, because we define our belief system from the Bible.

> However, when **He**, the Spirit of truth, has come **He** will guide you into all truth; for **He** will not speak of His own *authority,* but whatever **He** hears **He** will speak; and **He** will tell you things to come. ~ *John 16:13 (NKJV)*

Jesus, in one verse, used the pronoun He, seven times to describe the Holy Spirit as a He, not an it. Once you understand the Holy Spirit is the third person of the Godhead, you can have a personal relationship and interact with Him. Like God the Father and Jesus, the Holy Spirit is a gentleman. Jesus told His disciples the following one of the last times He met with His disciples.

> Nevertheless I tell you the truth. It is to your advantage that I go away; for if I do not go away, the Helper will not come to you; but if I depart, I will send Him to you. ~ *John 16:7 (NKJV)*

One of the first words Jesus really uses to describe the person of the Holy Spirit is "helper." The word in the Greek is parakletos, which literally means to come alongside and help. If Jesus sent Him and said it was better that He left so the Holy Spirit could come, you can be sure the Holy Spirit is trustworthy and very much like Jesus in nature. He certainly is not to be feared. Unfortunately, He's gotten a bad rap in certain circles where He has been misrepresented.

Unlike Jesus, who was confined to a human body while He was on earth, the Holy Spirit can be everywhere and be with everyone at the same time. He is truly your helper and guide. So, how does the Holy Spirit communicate with you?

Here are four tests you can use to determine if what you're hearing is truly the voice of the Holy Spirit.

1. The first test is this: The Holy Spirit is consistent. He will never contradict Himself or the Word of God.

> "I am the Lord, and I do not change." ~ *Malachi 3:6 (NLT)*

Sometimes people feel that they receive a special exception to what God has already said in the Bible. Here is what Scripture says about this: there are no exceptions that allow for violating Scripture. Notice, God feels so strongly about this the Scripture repeats it a second time.

> But even if we, or an angel from heaven, preach any other gospel to you than what we have preached to you, let him be [a] accursed. As we have said before, so now I say again, if anyone preaches any other gospel to you than what you have received, let him be accursed. ~ *Galatians 1:8-9 (NKJV)*

2. The Holy Spirit will lead you with peace, not pressure. Jesus is not a cattle rancher driving us,

65

and we're not called cattle, the Bible calls us sheep. The Shepherd goes out in front of the sheep and leads them with His voice. He'll direct us with His rod and staff, but He'll lead us with peace.

> "For you shall go out in joy, and be led out in peace." ~ *Isaiah 55:12 (NKJV)*

When you begin to lose your peace in a situation, it's time to slow down and pause, and ask, "Lord, are you trying to get my attention? What is it that you're wanting to say?" The Holy Spirit will never lead you through pressure.

3. He leads with conviction, not condemnation.

Jesus said,

> And when He, (speaking of the Holy Spirit) has come, He will convict the world of sin, and of righteousness, and of the judgment. ~ *John 16:8 (NKJV)*

It is that strong feeling of, "This is wrong, and this is right." It is called conviction. Satan and our mind will often condemn us. The Bible tells you God does not correct through condemnation.

> *There is* therefore now no condemnation to those who are in Christ Jesus. ~ *Romans 8:1 (NKJV)*

Everyone sins at times, and this is what the Bible encourages you to do regarding any sin in your life.

> If we confess our sins, He is faithful and just to forgive us *our* sins and to cleanse us from all unrighteousness. ~ *1 John 1:9 (NKJV)*

The Holy Spirit convicts you that what you did was wrong, and here's what conviction says, "You know that you're better than this. You're a child of God. You're the righteousness of God in Christ. You're a new creation. Get up, and let's get back on the horse, and try again." **Conviction inspires you to be better and to do better.**

Condemnation says, "Look at you, look at your sin. You are your sin. You are what you did." The Holy Spirit never condemns. In Christ Jesus, you're not what you did, you are what Jesus Christ did. It's not your sin that defines you it's His grace and salvation that defines you. Conviction says, "Get up." Condemnation says, "You don't deserve to get up." **Conviction gives you motivation to change. Condemnation brings a feeling of defeat.**

4. The Holy Spirit will always be clear, never confusing. The voice of the Holy Spirit and the working and moving of the Holy Spirit will always bring clarity; it will never bring confusion.

> For God is not *the author* of confusion, but
> of peace. ~ *1 Corinthians 14:33 (NKJV)*

This whole chapter talks about the working of the Holy Spirit and the gifts of the Spirit in the church. What we see repeatedly is that **God never brings confusion** into a situation. In fact, the opposite is true. When the Holy Spirit is at work and moving, He brings clarity. If someone ever tells you they have a word from God for you, and after you hear it, you feel confused, chances are it was not from God.

Another way you hear the Holy Spirit is by the inward voice of the Holy Spirit. The inward voice feels more authoritative and is usually very strong. It often seems like someone behind you said something, but when you turn around no one is there. You're tempted to say, "Woah! Who just said that?" It grabs your attention, where the witness is more like a sense or impression. In Acts 16 the Apostle Paul is planning to take the Gospel into Asia. Here we see an example of the inward voice.

> Now when they had gone through Phrygia and the region of Galatia, they were forbidden by the Holy Spirit to preach the word in Asia. After they had come to Mysia, they tried to go into Bithynia, but the Spirit did not permit them. So passing by Mysia, they came down to Troas. ~ *Acts 16:6-8 (NKJV)*

fresh start

Now, when they got there, Paul was wondering, "Why can't I go here and here?" The answer? The Holy Spirit had a better plan and wanted to direct them to another location. That night Paul saw a vision, while he slept, of a man in Macedonia saying, "Hey, come over here and help us." As you follow the story in Acts, what you'll see is the church at Philippi is birthed as Paul follows that vision, and a lot of great things take place because of his obedience. The gospel would ultimately get into Asia, but God had a different plan and sequence for Paul. The Lord used this authoritative inward voice. Notice the strong language. "He forbade, and did not permit us," which is a much stronger leading than just a sense of peace.

Now, unfortunately, there are a lot of Christians who actually get to Heaven sooner than they were supposed to because they ignored the peace of God, or the inward voice of the Holy Spirit. They meant well, but unfortunately, it was an opportunity for the enemy to take them out simply because they didn't listen to the leading of the Holy Spirit. This answers a lot of questions that many people have. "They were a good person, why did they go to Heaven so soon?" Sometimes, it's as simple as they just ignored the inward voice of God. Unfortunately, they suffered the consequences of it.

The Holy Spirit is your helper and guide in your Christian walk. He wants to draw you closer to Jesus and to God's highest and best for your life.

69

For a more in-depth look into this important topic, please watch Pursuit of Jesus Volume 1-The Holy Spirit-Videos 7-0 through 7-4.

Chapter 7

What's Next?

Church

Make a commitment to yourself to attend church regularly. The book of Acts is all about the formation of the church. Most of the first believers met daily. In our culture, most churches meet on the weekend.

> They worshiped together at the Temple each day, met in homes for the Lord's Supper, and shared their meals with great joy and generosity. ~ *Acts 2:46 (NLT)*

The church is much more than a building. A church is a community and family of believers. Everyone needs to feel a part of something bigger than themselves. The church in the Bible is often referred to as the body of Christ. Now that you are a believer, you're part of His body. It is important for you to plug into church. You'll find it is your lifeline. The Bible tells you not to neglect meeting together with other believers.

> And let us not neglect our meeting together, as some people do, but encourage one another, especially now

that the day of his return is drawing near.
~ *Hebrews 10:25 (NLT)*

The church is place for you to grow in your knowledge of God and have fellowship with like-minded people. It is also a place of safety. God wants to protect you as you grow in Him. He knows there is strength in numbers and protection. He also knows it is easy to get side-tracked or to drift; being part of the church creates accountability. The Bible often refers to us as sheep. Ironically, sheep have an enemy, wolves, and as God's sheep we have an enemy too. His name is Satan or the devil. The irony is both these enemies use exactly the same tactic to destroy their prey. If they can get one of the sheep separated from the safety of the flock, they can pick it off. Jesus wants you in the safety of the flock. His plans for you are to give you a life of significance and the enemy wants to derail that plan.

> The thief's purpose is to steal and kill and destroy. My purpose is to give them a rich and satisfying life. ~ *John 10:10 (NLT)*

So why is this important? The church reveals Jesus on the earth, like Jesus revealed God when He was on earth. As believers, we represent Jesus to a lost and hurting world. The church is where we learn to know Christ, grow in Christ, and show Christ.

Sharing

> Then the angel spoke to the women.
> "Don't be afraid!" he said. "I know you are
> looking for Jesus, who was crucified. He
> isn't here! He is risen from the dead, just
> as he said would happen. Come, see
> where his body was lying. And now, go
> quickly and tell his disciples that he has
> risen from the dead, and he is going
> ahead of you to Galilee. You will see him
> there. Remember what I have told you."
> ~ *Matthew 28:5-7 (NLT)*

The Gospel can be summarized in COME, SEE, GO, and TELL.

I once read that a person will lead more people
to Christ in their first year as a believer than in
the entire rest of their life combined. Why is that?

First, the chances are, most of your friends were
like you and didn't know Christ.

Second, your life change has a dramatic effect on
your old friends. They see the change in you.

Third, most Christians over time get comfortable
and forget what it was like without Christ, and
then we lose our zeal for evangelism.

> One day as Jesus was walking along the
> shore of the Sea of Galilee, he saw Simon
> [a] and his brother Andrew throwing a net
> into the water, for they fished for a living.

> Jesus called out to them, "Come, follow
> me, and I will show you how to fish for
> people!" And they left their nets at once
> and followed him. ~ *Mark 1:16-18 (NLT)*

We would expect Jesus to say, "Follow me and I will make you more disciplined, spiritual, smarter, or more organized," but instead He said He'd make them fishermen.

To follow is to fish. If I don't fish, "Who am I following?"

Sharing is simply telling others your story, telling them what Jesus did for you. You don't have to be a Biblical scholar to do that. All you need to know is, I believed Jesus died for my sins, and then I confessed Him with my mouth, and He changed my life. Then, fill it in with your own story.

Communion

As Christians, we have two holy sacraments that are memorials: communion and baptism. These are both celebrations of our new life in Christ.

Communion is a powerful way that you can know Christ in a more tangible way. Let's look at what the elements of communion truly mean. The Apostle Paul demonstrates communion in his letter to the Corinthian church.

> For I pass on to you what I received from
> the Lord himself. On the night when he

was betrayed, the Lord Jesus took some bread and gave thanks to God for it. Then he broke it in pieces and said, "This is my body, which is given for you. Do this in remembrance of me." ~ *1 Corinthians 11:23-24 (NLT)*

The Body

Have you ever thought, "If only I could just touch Jesus." "If I could just feel Him." Well, you can. Let's look at the above scripture again to explore this.

For I pass on to you what I received from the Lord himself. On the night when he was betrayed, the Lord Jesus took some bread and gave thanks to God for it. Then he broke it in pieces and said, "This is my body, which is given for you. [a] Do this in remembrance of me." ~ *1 Corinthians 11: 23-24 (NLT)*

Communion is a way we can touch the Lord's body. The bread represents His body.

We need to understand a few things about the Jewish setting of Passover where Jesus introduced this idea of communion for His New Testament followers. Jesus said that when you're holding the bread, it represents His broken body. In the Jewish culture, the bread He used would have been matza, an unleavened bread. Unleavened is a picture of being sinless. You'll

75

see throughout Scripture that leaven represents sin. When you put leaven in dough, it spreads through the entire dough and causes it to rise. That's what sin does. It starts out small, but it begins to permeate the rest of your life. The bread Jesus used was unleavened because Jesus was the sinless substitute for you. This bread had three distinctive characteristics and was used during Passover.

The first characteristic was that one side was burned. Why? This is a picture of the Passover lamb that was burned at the altar. It is a picture of an innocent lamb absorbing the wrath and judgement of God, being burned as a sacrifice for sin. Jesus is our sinless substitute, the Lamb of God. When He hung on the cross, all God's fiery wrath and indignation that you and I deserved as sinners was poured out on Jesus Christ. He took the judgment that we deserved.

Second, the other side of the bread was pierced. The Bible tells us that the body of Jesus Christ was pierced. In fact, there were seven different puncture wounds in Christ's body. In Scripture, seven is the number of completion. When Jesus was pierced seven times, it was a complete sacrifice for our healing.

Third, there were stripes on the side that was pierced as well, because Jesus was whipped. Before His crucifixion, the Roman soldiers tied him to a post, stripped Him of His clothing, and whipped Him with a "Cat of Nine Tails." This whip had beads of metal and broken glass on the end of it. The soldiers would whip the back of someone, and they would pull it back, and it would literally begin to peel off the layers of skin and then layers of flesh. Forty lashes was known to kill someone, so they would take them right up to the point of death with 39 lashes and stop just to keep them alive. It was a very, very cruel form of torture. When Jesus was beaten and flogged, they did that to Him, and the Bible tells us why in a prophesy about Jesus in the book of Isaiah.

> But He was wounded for our transgressions, He was bruised for our iniquities; The chastisement of our peace was upon Him, And by His stripes we are healed. ~ *Isaiah 53:5 (NKJV)*

In 1 Peter 2:24, Peter quotes this Scripture and says, 'by His stripes, or wounds, we are healed." As a Christ follower, as you take the elements of communion you're not just going through a ritual, you're remembering that Jesus provided for your healing. First, for your salvation, but you also needed healing for your mental and emotional health; we all came from some sort of dysfunction. His stripes also paid for your physical healing as well. Whatever healing it is you are in need of in your life, when you take the elements of communion, thank Him that you're healed in every area that needs healing. When you realize what all this means, it makes the presence of Christ in your life very real.

When we take the bread, we are taking healing for every part of our life.

Why do we start communion with the body? We invite Jesus in, and then He cleans us up.

The Blood

Now, let's talk about the blood of Jesus Christ that He shed for us, and this powerful symbolic element of communion. Here's what Jesus said in Matthew 26:27-28.

> And he took a cup of wine and gave thanks to God for it. He gave it to them and said, "Each of you drink from it, for this is my blood, which confirms the covenant between God and his people. It is poured out as a sacrifice to forgive the sins of many." ~ *Matthew 26:27-28 (NLT)*

Jesus didn't just come to cover your sins; He removed them. In the Old Testament, when a lamb was sacrificed for the sins of the people, it covered their sins. However, in the New Testament Jesus' sacrifice brought complete removal of your sins. The Bible uses the term "justified." You are justified in Christ Jesus. I love one definition of this, it's "just if I never sinned."

So, when you drink the juice that represents the shed blood of Jesus Christ, what you're saying is, "Lord, I believe that you died for every sin. I thank you that there's power in the blood of Jesus to cleanse my sins." The blood of Jesus completely sets me free from the power of sin.

The Apostle Paul said in the Book of Romans,

> Sin is no longer your master, for you no longer live under the requirements of the law. Instead, you live under the freedom of God's grace. ~ *Romans 6:14 (NLT)*

This grace that you've been given through the shed blood of Jesus Christ cleanses you and sets you free from sin. Why is the blood so significant? In the Old Testament in the Book of Leviticus, God explained to His people why the blood's so important.

> For the life of the body is in its blood. ~ *Leviticus 17:11 (NLT)*

This was recorded in the Bible thousands of years before scientists would discover that life is truly in the blood. This validates the authenticity of God's Word.

When you look into the Old Testament you will see that Israel would sacrifice a spotless lamb without blemish to cover their sins. You might think that it is not fair that a little lamb who had nothing wrong would be killed for someone else's sins and you're not wrong. It isn't fair and that's exactly the point. Jesus, the sinless lamb of God, was put to death for your sin and my sin. That is not fair.

People often say, "I want God to be fair." No, you don't! If God were fair, we would die for our sins rather than Jesus. God is merciful and gracious. God is also just; in that He has to punish sin. For those who accept Christ's sacrifice, they are free from His punishment. However, those who reject His sacrifice will face the judgement they deserve.

When you drink the juice at communion, this should fill your heart with gratitude for Jesus, your Savior, and make you desire to live a godly life.

> But if we confess our sins to him, he is faithful and just to forgive us our sins and to cleanse us from all wickedness. ~ *1 John 1:9 (NLT)*

When we take communion, we confess sin and receive His forgiveness.

You may be thinking, "I've messed up too much and been too bad for God to forgive me!

There is an interesting note to this story. The lamb for the sacrifice was to have no broken bones. Jesus' bones were not broken when He hung on the cross. Why is this important? Blood is produced in the bone marrow, because His bones were not broken there is an endless supply. His mercies are new every morning.

Baptism

If you are a new believer, or have recently rededicated your life to the Lord, your next step is to be baptized. This is how we show the world that we have a changed life. Jesus set an example for us in this and one of the last instructions He left with His disciples was this.

> "Therefore, go and make disciples of all the nations, baptizing them in the name of the Father and the Son and the Holy Spirit." ~ *Matthew 28:19 (NLT)*

If baptism was included in His final instructions, it's important. Baptism is a step of obedience in your walk with Christ. Baptism does not save you. It's a symbol and celebration of your new life in Christ. It is an outward expression of an inward change.

> For you were buried with Christ when you were baptized. And with him you were raised to new life because you trusted the mighty power of God, who raised Christ from the dead. ~ *Colossians 2:12 (NLT)*

As you go down under the water, you are saying publicly, "I have died to my old life." When you come up out of the water, you are declaring, "I have been raised to my new life in Christ, I am a changed person."

The book of Acts contains a story about a man named Phillip who was an evangelist. God instructed him to go down a certain road and help an Ethiopian eunuch who held a high office understand what he was reading from the Bible in the book of Isaiah. The eunuch was returning from Jerusalem where he went to worship God. He was a Gentile, an outsider, and someone who would not usually be accepted in the Jewish culture. Then, God intervened in his life and sent Phillip to him. God meets you where you are. Phillip jumped into his carriage with him and explained the Scriptures he was reading. They were all about Jesus and as the man heard about Jesus, the Messiah, he believed.

> As they rode along, they came to some water, and the eunuch said, "Look! There's some water! Why can't I be baptized?" He ordered the carriage to stop, and they went down into the water, and Philip baptized him. When they came up out of the water, the Spirit of the Lord snatched Philip away. The eunuch never saw him again but went on his way rejoicing. ~ *Acts 8:36-39 (NLT)*

Baptism is also a declaration of our commitment to follow Jesus. This is like my wedding ring. I stood at the altar and made covenant vows with my wife, and then she put my wedding ring on my finger. If I take my ring off it doesn't make me divorced, because it wasn't the ring that made me married, it was the covenant vows my wife and I made to one another. You can't just go to a store, buy a wedding ring, and say I'm married.

In the same way, it is not baptism that saves you. It was believing in your heart and confessing Jesus as Lord that saved you. Baptism is like the wedding ring. It is a sign of your commitment to Jesus.

Baptism is also a demonstration of change.

> This means that anyone who belongs to Christ has become a new person. The old life is gone; a new life has begun! ~ 2 Corinthians 5:17 (NLT)

Tradition says that years before we had heated indoor baptismal, people got baptized in the river. They put on pure white clothing and then over the top of those clothes put on dirty tattered clothes. When the pastor dipped them under the water, they would rip off the dirty tattered clothing and let it float down the river. When they came up out of the water they were in their spotless pure white clothes. This was a picture of them letting the old life go washed away by Christ and the beginning of their new life in Christ. This is a great picture of what happens to us spiritually.

> Well then, should we keep on sinning so that God can show us more and more of his wonderful grace? Of course not! Since

> we have died to sin, how can we continue to live in it? Or have you forgotten that when we were joined with Christ Jesus in baptism, we joined him in his death? For we died and were buried with Christ by baptism. And just as Christ was raised from the dead by the glorious power of the Father, now we also may live new lives. ~ *Romans 6:1-4 (NLT)*

When we gave our lives to Christ, we were born again. We figuratively died with Christ and were given a new life and wonderful life in Christ. Baptism is an outward picture of that inward change.

I often get asked about infant baptism. I don't see that in Scripture. What I do see is baby dedication. The people in the Bible would bring their child to the Temple to be dedicated to the Lord. Joseph and Mary took baby Jesus to the temple for dedication. You can read that story in the book of Luke 2:22-34.

Many have also asked should I get rebaptized if I was baptized as an infant? Your parents had great intentions for you. We celebrate baby dedication at Element. However, if you were not a believer when you were baptized, you choosing to be baptized as a believer is the ultimate fulfillment of your parent's intention. It is not dishonoring, but honoring.

I encourage you to take this next step in your spiritual journey with getting baptized in your local church. If you are local, we look forward to celebrating your new life in Christ with you at your baptism in the near future. You can register at: https://www.elementchurch.com/baptism-registration/.

Serving

> God saved you by his grace when you believed. And you can't take credit for this; it is a gift from God. Salvation is not a reward for the good things we have done, so none of us can boast about it. For we are God's masterpiece. He has created us anew in Christ Jesus, so we can do the good things he planned for us long ago. ~ *Ephesians 2:8-10 (NLT)*

A masterpiece is something of great value. You are worth far more to God than any earthly masterpiece ever made by a man. God saved you by His grace, because you have great value. You were saved by grace for good works. God created you for a purpose with gifts and talents that are meant to be shared. A life of significance is a life that includes giving of yourself to serve others.

That word, created, in the Greek, gives the idea of proprietorship of the manufacturer. It's the idea of something being copyrighted or patented and trademarked.

> God has given each of you a gift from his great variety of spiritual gifts. Use them well to serve one another. ~ *1 Peter 4:10 (NLT)*

What we do with the cross determines WHERE we spend eternity. The way we live now determines HOW we will live in eternity.

> For we must all stand before Christ to be judged. We will each receive whatever we deserve for the good or evil we have done in this earthly body. ~ *2 Corinthians 5:10 (NLT)*

We are going to appear before the judgment seat of Christ. The Greek word here for judgment seat is Bema. It means a rostrum, or a raised platform to receive an award. This is much like what Olympians stand on to receive their medals.

> "And God will wipe away every tear from their eyes; there shall be no more death, nor sorrow, nor crying. There shall be no more pain, for the former things have passed away." ~ *Revelation 21:4 (NKJV)*

Why will God wipe away every tear if there are no more tears in Heaven? I agree with many Bible scholars who believe when we stand before God and see what we had the potential to do but didn't, there will be tears. The good news is that God will wipe them all away. There is a famous quote by Les Brown about the graveyard being the richest place on earth.

> "The graveyard is the richest place on earth, because it is here that you will find all the hopes and dreams that were never fulfilled, the books that were never written, the songs that were never sung, the inventions that were never shared, the cures that were never discovered, all because someone was too afraid to take that first step, keep with the problem, or determined to carry out their dream." ~ *Les Brown*

Don't let this be your legacy, determine to find your purpose and fulfill your calling. Live a life of no regrets. When you were born again, you do a do over. Make it count. This is the legacy God has for you.

> For I know the thoughts that I think toward you, says the Lord, thoughts of peace and not of evil, to give you a future and a hope. Then you will call upon Me and go and pray to Me, and I will listen to you. And you will seek Me and find *Me*, when you search for Me with all your heart. ~ *Jeremiah 29:11-13 (NKJV)*

One of the best ways to begin your new legacy is to start serving in the local church. This gives you an opportunity to use your gifts, make like-minded friends, and experience the joy and fulfillment which come in making a difference in the lives of others. I strongly encourage you to get connected with one of our serve teams. We will walk along side of you to help you find just the right fit. If you are not in our local area, reach out to your local church to get involved.

About the Author

Erik Lawson is the founding pastor of Element Church, a congregation of more than 5,000 with its main campus located in Wentzville, Missouri. He is known for his dynamic communication style and in-depth Bible teaching communicated with practical life application. In addition to his role as the senior pastor of a multi-site local church, and a world-wide online presence with Element Everywhere, he has an insightful leadership podcast called *All Out Leadership* and is a one-on-one leadership coach to pastors.

Prior to founding Element Church he led what was at the time, the largest youth group in America, Church on The Move's nationally acclaimed, Oneighty©, with as many as 3,000 young people attending each week.

Erik lives in Wentzville, Missouri with his wife Sunny and their dog Flash. He is the father of three wonderful adult children and has two beautiful granddaughters. In his free time, Erik enjoys spending time reading, playing Fortnite with friends, going for walks in the park with Sunny, and eating ice cream.

www.ingramcontent.com/pod-product-compliance
Lightning Source LLC
Chambersburg PA
CBHW060342050426
42449CB00011B/2814